Beautiful In Bones

Beautiful In Bones

Caterina Imbro

Tragic Thespians

'Beautiful in Bones' by Caterina Imbro

ISBN: 978-0-646-89960-2

Illustration & Text: Caterina Imbro

Dedications:

To my loving husband, Ryan, who allowed me to set free the words in my heart.

To my family, friends, lovers and enemies who inspired my creativity and passion.

"All women become like their mothers.
That is their tragedy. No man does. That's his."
-Oscar Wilde

Table of contents

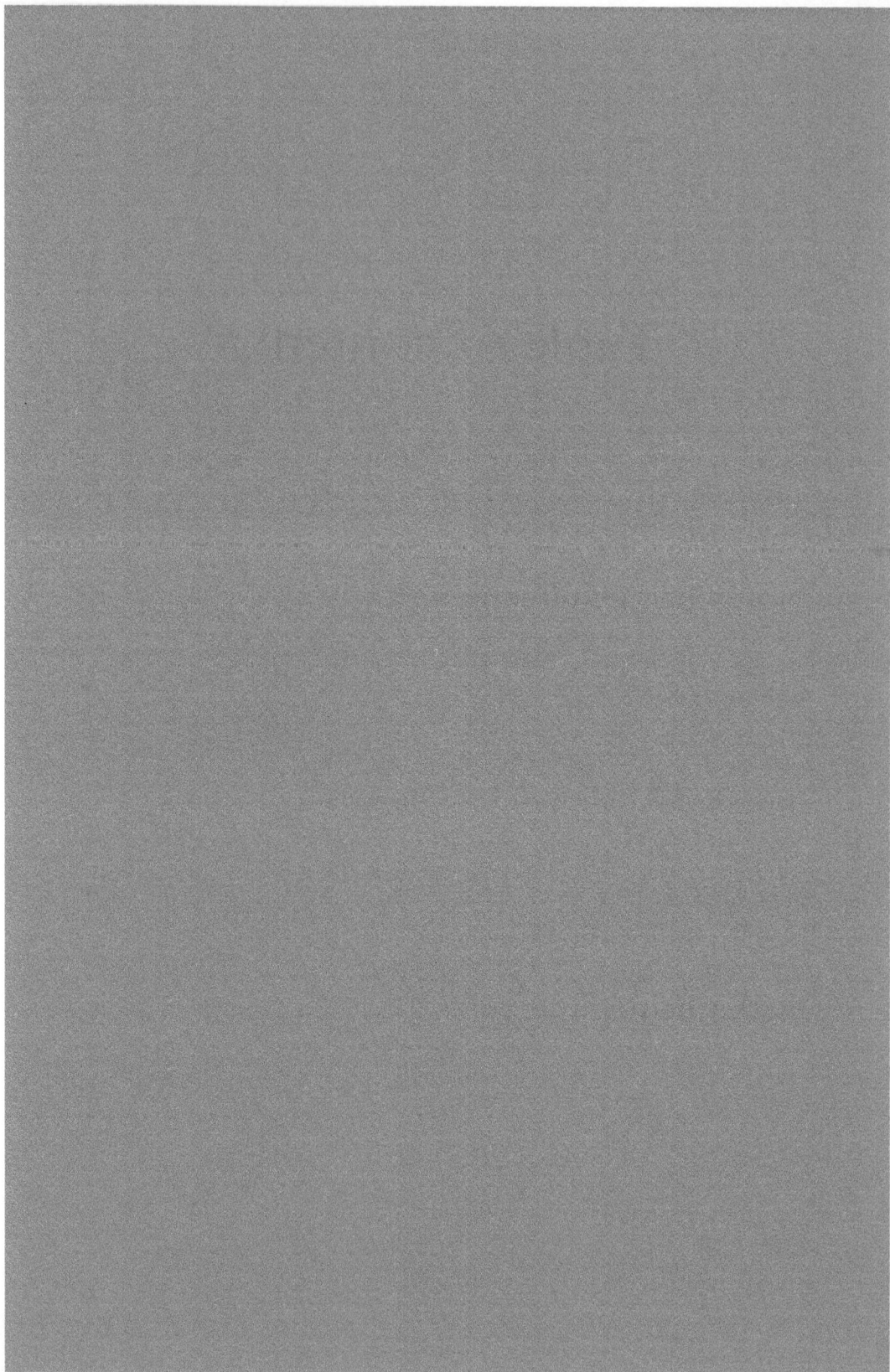

Roots

THE GENESIS WITHIN

The Tongue Of Time

In the whispers of my father's voice,

Echoes weave, a timeless choice,

Melodies of heritage and pride,

Yet distant to me, on life's swift tide.

Guilt threads through each passing day,

Where familiar words in my native tongue play,

While another language softly sings,

Fading like a distant bell that rings.

I ponder often, in silent musing,

The gap between us, subtly bruising,

His native tongue, deeply entwined,

Foreign still within my mind.

In childhood's haven, innocence finds,

I embraced my tongue, where my heart binds,

Yet with each passing year, a subtle regret,

That another tongue I did not beget.

For languages carry tales untold,

Roots deep within ancestral hold,

Though I wander from that shore,

Its absence in me resonates more.

But in this guilt, resolve takes root,
To bridge the gap, heal the mute,
To learn, to cherish, to reclaim,
The essence of that lost refrain.

Though tongues may part, our spirits entwine,
Beyond words, a passion divine,
In spirit, in bond, we remain aligned,
Through memories, through tenderness enshrined.

So, father, pardon this linguistic cleft,
In love's hold, no divide is left,
Together we'll journey, hand in hand,
Tracing language's thread across the land.

Mother

In the quiet corners of memories

A mother and daughter once shared a sacred plea,

Connected by whispers and laughter's bright gleam,

Their bond a tapestry woven from dreams.

In childhood's signet, they danced hand in hand,

A duo of hearts in a whimsical land,

Where love bloomed freely, without restraint,

Each day a canvas of joy and quaint.

But time's swift currents, they did not foresee,

Tugged at their ties, a tempest at sea,

As adolescence dawned with its turbulent wave,

Words turned to weapons, and valour couldn't save.

The daughter's path twisted, ventured astray,

Her mother's words cut like daggers each day,

Misunderstandings grew roots deep and wide,

Their bond fractured, pain locked inside.

Years wore on, wounds festered in shadow's keep,

Until maturity whispered, a promise to reap,

In life's ebb and flow, where currents entwine,

The daughter sought solace, a fragment of time.

She reached out tentatively, seeking to mend,

Bridges left shattered, with time to transcend.

And in the mother's eyes, she saw mirrored there,

A little girl's hopes, a mother's care.

Through tears that fell, and laughter that soared,

They rebuilt the bridge, fragile yet restored,

The daughter learned, with a courage now grown,

Her mother, too, had fantasies of her own.

Once a little girl, yearning to play,

To be loved and cherished in her own gentle way,

To dream of tomorrow and succeed,

With parental approval, her heart to heed.

Their wounds became stories etched in time's scroll,

Love's tender healing made their bond whole,

A beat of the heart, sharing each day's embrace,

In refuge, finding solace and grace.

For life's intricate dance, where paths may diverge,

The bond of a mother and daughter, they merge,

Through trials and triumphs, they come to see,

Love's enduring strength, its eternal decree.

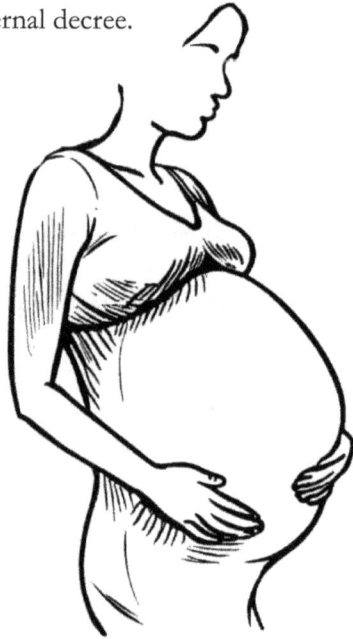

Terra Madre

Nella terra che ha dato vita ai miei antenati,

mi sento un ramo spezzato, nato altrove,

cresciuta

 diversamente, con una vita e una lingua

che i miei progenitori non avrebbero potuto immaginare.

Colpevolezza mi avvolge come nebbia mattutina,

misto a un amore profondo per questa madre patria,

che ha plasmato le radici del mio essere,

anche se il mio cammino è stato su sentieri lontani.

Gli occhi degli avi brillano nei miei sogni,

e sento il richiamo delle antiche colline e dei mari,

mentre il passato danza con il presente

nella danza incerta della mia identità divisa.

Ogni parola che pronuncio, ogni passo che faccio,

porta il peso di un'eterna nostalgia e gratitudine,

per la terra che ha nutrito il mio sangue e il mio spirito,

nonostante le distanze che ci separano ora.

Ma nel cuore rimane un legame indissolubile,

un amore senza tempo per la madre che ho conosciuto solo attraverso storie,

che mi ha dato luce, anche se il sole splende altrove,

e mi insegna a navigare il mare della mia dualità.

Così, anche se sono un ramo spezzato,

so che appartengo a questa terra che chiamo casa,

dove il passato si fonde con il presente

e il mio cuore batte al ritmo di un amore senza fine.

The Cradle Of Life

The cradle of life's tender light,

Mother and child, a bond so bright,

Once entangled as one, heart to heart,

In a dance of devotion's enduring art.

From the first flutter, a shared heartbeat,

Reverberates pure and sweet,

in whispers and lullabies'

their souls are gently tied.

But time, unforgiving in its flow,

guides them on paths they come to know,

like ships passing in the night,

like whispers lost in the twilight.

Days unfold, a journey of growth,

Guided by a mother's faithful oath.

Guiding, nurturing, with tender care,

Through laughter, tears, in joys they share.

Yet in the cycle, destined and true,

A day may come when skies don't turn blue,

When paths diverge, and roles must change,

An inevitable parting, heartaches arrange.

For life's seasons shift, as they must,

Mother's hold, a bittersweet trust,

In memories cherished and eternally kept,

A legacy where tears are wept.

Though the day may dawn, when she must part,

Child carries within, mother's heart,

For love transcends earthly refrain,

In souls united, forever remain.

We Were Girls Together

We were girls together,

In the golden hours of innocence,

Arms intertwined, we chased the sun,

Imaginations wild and a world full of fun,

Secrets shared in whispers light,

Underneath the stars of night.

From skipping ropes to whispered crushes,

In childhood games, our friendship rushes,

Through playgrounds where we used to roam,

We forged a bond, a place called home.

But time, relentless in its flight,

Led us on separate paths, out of sight,

From carefree days to grown-up dreams,

Life unfolded in unforeseen streams.

Yet still, in moments of quiet reflection,

I see your smile, feel the connection,

For though we've grown and life's unfurled,

We carry with us that shared girlhood world.

In the tapestry of our memories, forever woven,

The laughter, the tears, the love unbroken,

Side by side, through joy and weathered storm,

We were girls together, now women strong.

Bow Down

From cradle to my throne, courage foretold.

Through trials and triumphs, my spirit bold.

With my sceptre of truth, sharp and keen,

Resilience, my crown, fit for any queen.

In this realm where strength and mercy entwine,

By choice I reign, my path defined.

Tall amid trials, unbowed, unshaken,

A queen in every kingdom, never mistaken.

So, when mighty grandeur comes my way,

With unwavering command, I say:

Bow down to the queen of this domain,

Ruler of my fate, freedom's reign.

Missing Piece

I'm a puzzle, intricate and unsolved,
Finding humor in the numbness, unresolved.
Each piece I fit, a step in the unknown,
Yet the more I assemble, the less I'm shown.

I'm a song, melodies left unsung,
Oddly loud, yet unnoticed among some.
My words reverberate, but fall on deaf ears,
A silent choir, lost in silent fears.

I'm a shadow, devoid of light
Shapeless, unseen, lost from sight.
No way to reveal my true form,
Lost in what I am, adrift and torn.

In Another Life

I often wonder, I ponder deep,
If time spun back, would our paths meet?
Would we laugh together over silly jokes,
Or share secrets under the whispering oaks?

If we were peers, would she understand
The dreams I chase, the shifting sands.
Would she see me, unmasked and true,
Or would her gaze pierce, unsure and askew?

In another life, would she be my guide,
Through trials and triumphs, side by side?
Would we bond over music and books,
Or exchange knowing glances, wordless looks?

I wonder if her wisdom would shine bright,
A beacon of hope in the darkest night.
Would she cherish my quirks, my every flaw,
Or would distance linger, an unyielding maw?

My Home On Margaret Way

The walls grow colder, a chill in the air,

Time slips by, leaving strands of despair.

I'm getting older, each day a step,

In this house that once held relics we kept.

A house is not a home, I now understand,

Without the warmth of touch, a guiding hand.

Ghosts linger in the corridors, memories unfold,

Whispers of laughter, stories retold.

Imprint of footsteps, traces on the floor,

In these quiet moments, I yearn for more.

The past haunts these halls, a silence vast,

A loss that time cannot outlast.

Faded photographs, frames on the wall,

Capture moments, both big and small.

But the anguish remains, a lingering ache,

For the home we built, now adrift and opaque.

To My Child Self

Dear little one beneath the olive tree,

Where dreams were bright, wild and free,

Your tender roots in soft earth grew,

A world of wonder just for you.

The olive tree, so small and young,

With branches reaching, songs unsung,

Mirrors you in every way,

As seasons change and time gives way.

Though you've grown, and branches bend,

Remember where your story began.

In every leaf and every scar,

The essence of your youth is never far.

So to my child self, pure and bright,

Embrace the growth, the coming light.

For in the tree's enduring grace,

Your youthful spirit finds its place.

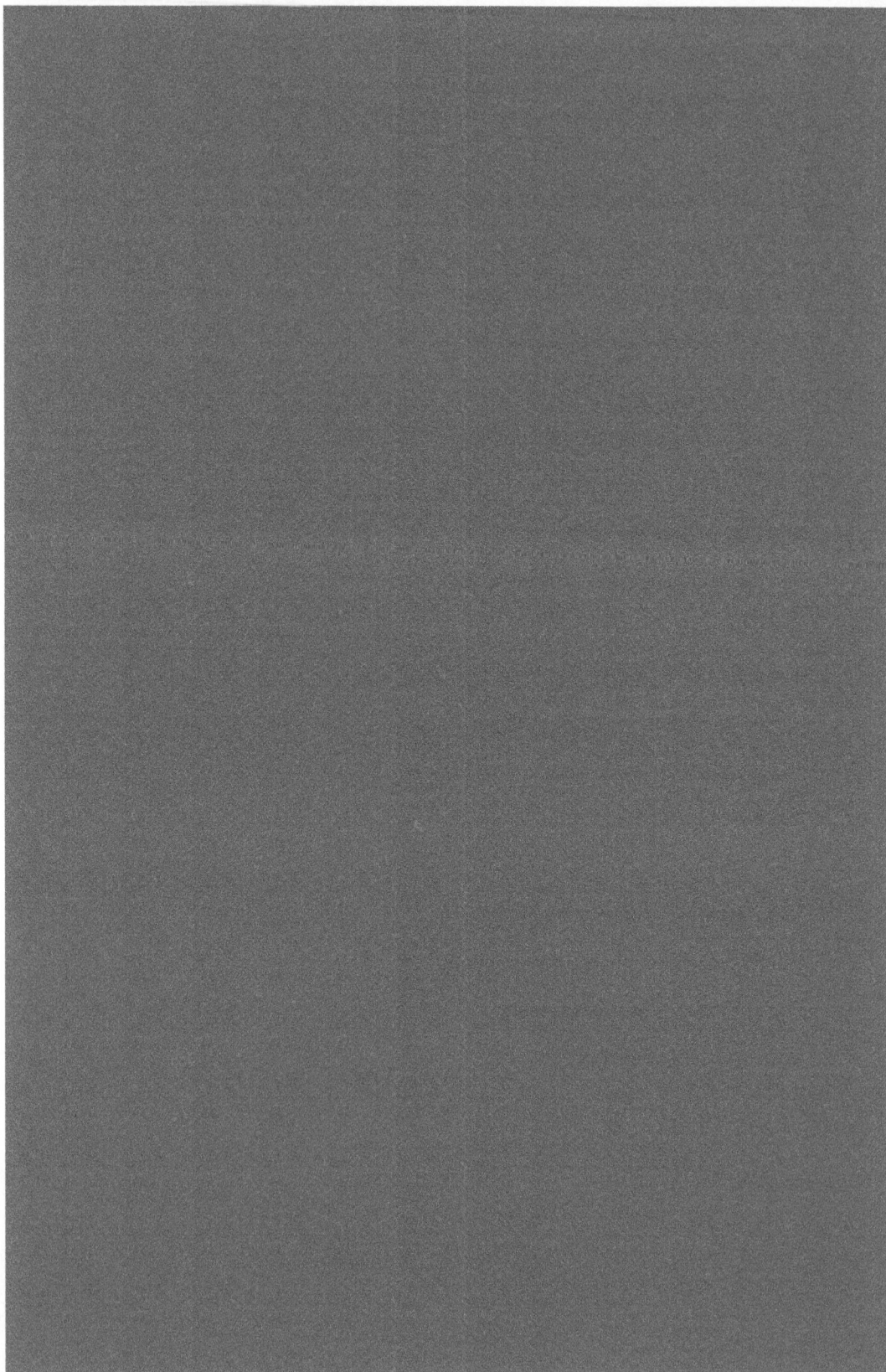

Mortality

EMBRACING IMPERMANENCE

Reflections On Mortality

Aching emptiness fills the void within,

A soul adrift, where do I begin?

For I feel the weight of time's cruel hand,

Drawing me closer to distant lands.

Terrified of the day I'll fade away,

Just a memory, a whisper's sway,

Will they remember who I used to be,

My thoughts, my deepest plea?

In the labyrinth of my stream of thought,

Where senses once lingered, now distraught,

I grasp at fragments of what once was mine,

No light in the tunnel, no beacon bright,

Only darkness lengthening into night,

As darkness wraps around me tight,

 I face the void, devoid of sight.

Alone, I ponder life's fleeting grasp,

How swiftly moments slip and pass,

Into the abyss, where all must wane,

Leaving behind a silent refrain.

In this quietude, I find no release,

Only echoes of pain that will not cease,

For in the end, all fades to gray,

And I, too, will quietly slip away.

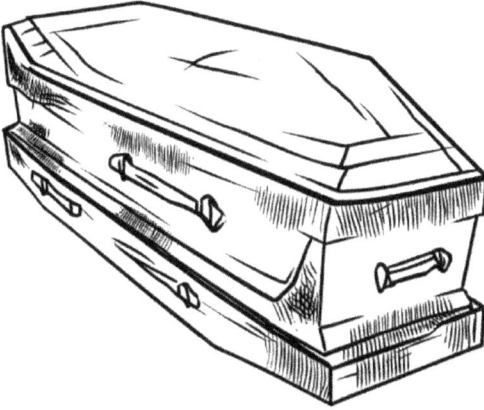

Mistress Of Death

In the gloom where the moonlight fades,

There walks a figure in the misty glades,

Her eyes like stars, her touch so cold,

She's Death's mistress, mysterious and bold.

Oh, Death's mistress, dancing in the night,

Whispering secrets in the pale moonlight,

She weaves her spell with a gentle caress,

Guiding souls to eternal rest.

In her eyes, the wisdom of the stars,

A guide through life's eternal scars.

She holds the keys to realms unseen,

A mistress of darkness, yet so serene.

Oh, Death's mistress, keeper of the keys,

In the silence, where the river meets the seas,

She holds the secrets of life's fleeting breath,

Her presence a tango between life and death.

She walks the path that few dare tread,

With a crown of stars upon her head,

A tender smile, a touch so kind,

She brings the solace that we all find.

With every step, a tale unfolds,

Of shattered hearts grown cold,

Her laughter echoes through the gloom,

A haunting melody in the silent room.

Oh, Death's mistress, keeper of the flame,

In the stillness, your name's a haunting claim.

She guides the weary to their final rest,

In her aura, we are truly blessed.

So, fear her not, this lady fair,

For she holds a beauty beyond compare,

In the dance of life, she plays her part,

Death's mistress, with a gentle heart.

Whispers Beyond

My heart yearns to ask questions that remain unsaid,

A whisper lost among the silence of the dead.

For those I loved and lost, in regions unseen,

I carry this unspoken query, like a sacred dream.

To you, dear departed, whose presence now fades,

In the veil between worlds, where silence pervades,

I yearn to ask of your journey, your unseen path,

In the aftermath of farewells, in the aftermath of wrath.

Did you find the peace you sought in life's fleeting dance?

Did warmth accompany you in your final glance?

Were there words left unspoken, regrets to be healed?

In the quiet of eternity, are wounds sealed?

Oh, how I long for just one more chance,

To bridge the divide, in a timeless trance,

To share a moment, to hold you near,

To erase the distance, to quell my fear.

But time's cruel decree has severed our conversation,

Leaving me with an unending sensation.

The emptiness of unanswered questions, a void so deep,

Leaves me longing for closure, for secrets to keep.

In the silence that stretches between us now,

I wonder if you hear my silent vow.

I cling to wondering how to find peace amidst this lingering ache,

To mend the heart that your absence does make.

For in the realm where your spirit now dwells,

I yearn to know the stories your silence tells.

Yet here I stand, with words unspoken,

lost in the quietude, a spirit broken.

Dear Nonna

Grandmother dear, in your silent repose,

A question lingers, I wonder if your spirit knows.

Do you feel the chill of earth's embrace,

Wrapped in solitude, in that sacred place?

Does the darkness comfort or bring you fear,

As you slumber in peace, far from here?

I imagine your hands, once warm and kind,

Now clasped in stillness, what thoughts cross your mind?

Are you aware of the tears we've shed,

Or the words left unspoken, heavy as lead?

The coffin, a vessel, now holds you tight,

Shielded from day, from morning's light.

But does it shield you from the cold, my dear,

Or do you linger in a chill that sears?

I whisper to the night, seeking emancipation in rhyme,

Hoping somehow, you'll hear me, across space and time.

For in the silence that follows your farewell,

My heart aches with questions, too heavy to expel.

Do you dream, grandmother, in that quiet still,

Of a warm place where love's light gently spills?

Or does the cold now claim your soul,

As I struggle to grasp this final toll?

In the late-night hours, thoughts wander deep,

To where you rest, in eternal sleep.

I hope you've found peace, beyond earthly pain,

In the cold of the coffin, or warmth regained.

Echoes of Absence

A presence vanished, a void in the heart,

Questions unanswered tear me apart.

Where have you gone, my wandering star?

In the vast expanse, lost yet not far.

Days stretch into nights, a persistent quest,

Tracing footsteps in memories' crest.

Each corner turned, each silhouette chased,

Hoping to find you, surrounded by grace.

The world is quiet, as if holding its breath,

Yearning for your return, praying for strength.

In the ache of absence, hope flickers dim,

A beacon searching from within.

For you are not lost, just somewhere unseen,

In the fabric of time, where imagines convene.

Until the day you're found, or whispers cease,

I'll hold your essence, in heart's release.

Possessions To The Grave

Is everything but a fleeting dream,

A flicker in life's passing stream?

The accolades, the trophies won,

In the void, do they all become undone?

We face the truth, stark and brave,

Can we carry wealth beyond the grave?

Golden idols, built to last, yet in the end, they crumble, fade,

Mere echoes in the darkened shade.

Not gold nor gems, nor fortunes vast,

Can defy the hourglass, steadfast.

For in the end, when all is said,

We take no treasures to the bed.

What use the riches, the grand display,

When death's cold hand takes all away?

The mansions built on shifting sands,

Lost in time's ruthless hands.

No marble tomb can house our dreams,

No worldly wealth redeems.

For what is worth, when life's unfurled,

In the void of the eternal world?

For in the quiet of the tomb

No treasures hold, no riches bloom.

No titles whispered in the dark,

No monuments, no worldly mark.

Into the abyss of time's cruel wave,

What remains of what we crave?

Forever 28

Where are you now?

Your presence a ghostly vow,

Once here, now gone,

Lost in shadows, withdrawn.

Another night, restless, torn apart,

Your absence grips, aching heart.

Taken too soon, I can't grasp why,

No words suffice, just tears that dry.

We never captured moments in frames,

Now memories flash, untamed.

I crave one last embrace, a touch,

But time slips by, asking too much.

Scattered thoughts in chaos array,

None of it fits, none can allay.

You were here, a vibrant light,

Now extinguished, day turned to night.

No answers soothe, no reasons found,

For snuffing out your flame, profound.

In our history, you reside,

Where grief and cherished moments coincide.

Your Instagram lingers, frozen in time,

A haunting reminder, a silent chime.

No new posts to fill the void,

Just memories we desperately avoid.

I'm scared to speak your name aloud,

A melody lost, no longer proud.

Sadness hangs heavy, sorrow deep,

No tomorrows, only grief's keep.

A year near passed, since you left,

Questions linger, last breath bereft.

What crossed your mind in that final sigh,

As life slipped away, without goodbye.

But the words Macbeth spoke, truth rings clear,

What's done can't be undone, no rear.

Your death, unfair, makes no sense,

Leaves us grappling, soul's defence.

through the pain, one truth remains,

Love transcends, your legacy sustains.

In our hearts, forever you'll stay,

Frozen in time, forever twenty-eight.

The Cross

Through hallowed halls where prayers would rise,
I found consolation in the stories, in the skies,
Each ritual a rhythm, a sacred dance,
Binding spirit and soul in divine trance.

But as the years unfolded, doubts took seed,
Questions whispered where certainty once agreed,
In the quiet corners of a searching mind,
I sought truths that faith had defined.

The world stretched wide, its complexities vast,
And faith's pillars faltered, weakened at last,
What once anchored me, began to slip away,
Leaving debris of doubt, in disarray.

No longer could I find solacement in prayer,
Or see the divine in the heavens' stare,
Beliefs that shaped me, now feel misplaced,
In the shifting sands where doubts are faced.

Yet in losing religion, a new path emerged,
A journey inward where wisdom surged,
In the depths of doubt, a truth profound,

That faith resides in the heart unbound.

For what shaped me in those early days,
Was not just the rituals, the hymns' praise,
But the values instilled, the affection that grew,
In compassion, in deeds I pursue.

So though religion's grip may have slipped away,
Leaving remnants of what once held sway,
I carry its essence, its teachings deep,
In the kindness I show, in the promises I keep.

For faith is not confined to sacred walls,
Nor bound by doctrine's rigid calls,
It lives in the spirit, in actions true,
In the empathy I offer, in the love I imbue.

In losing religion, I found a wider view,
A tapestry of beliefs, diverse and new,
And though the journey was marked by loss,
It led me to a faith that transcends the cross.

Incarnation

Turn to the skies, they say,

Bound and obey, follow the way.

Beg your God to end your hunger's strife,

Seek salvation in a higher life.

But no salvation comes from above,

In the depths of self, I find my love.

I am my own incarnation, bold and free,

Crafting my path, defining what will be.

No deity's hand guides my fate,

I shape my world, early or late.

In my flesh and bone, spirit entwined,

I define my truth, my peace of mind.

For in this life, in my creation,

I am my own, my own incarnation.

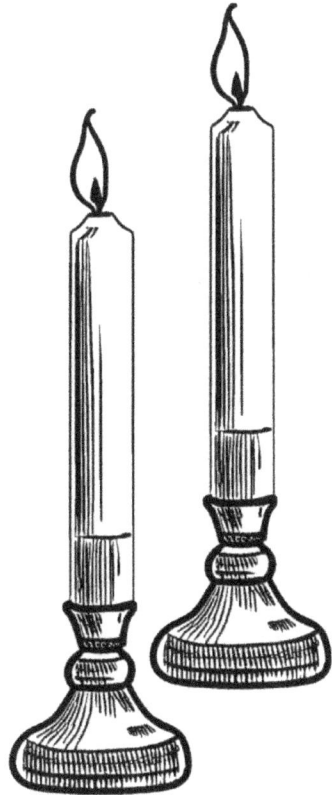

Blue Christmas

Singing "Blue Christmas" with a heavy heart,

Feeling the absence tear us apart.

The choir of laughter, cards in hand,

If only we knew it was our last stand.

Your voice in harmony, now a distant tune,

Memories flash like stars and the moon.

Each card played, a moment cherished dear,

Now etched in sorrow, crystal clear.

How quickly time slips through our grasp,

Leaving behind an ache that lasts.

In the game of life, the cards we drew,

Unaware it would end too soon.

I sing "Blue Christmas" with a tear,

For the moments lost, for you not here.

In every note, in every refrain,

I hold onto memories, despite the pain.

NEXT STOP

At the train station where tracks converge,
Life unfolds, its endless surge.
Each platform a stage, stories to unfold,
As journeys begin, as tales are told.

On one platform, youth's eager stride,
Faces aglow, hunger open wide.
Boundless hope in their eager eyes,
Adventure beckons under limitless skies.

Next stop, a platform where hearts align,
Tenderly entwined, in love's design.
Whispers shared in the midnight hour,
As a journey blooms like a fragile flower.

Further down, a platform worn and wise,
Faces etched with life's surprise.
Memories carried in weathered hands,
Lessons learned on distant lands.

And on another, children at play,
Innocence dancing, laughter's display.
Imaginations soar on youthful wings,

As the world outside softly sings.

Next stop, a platform of farewell's tear,
Partings whispered, moments dear.
Hands held tight in a final embrace,
As time's train moves at its own pace.

At every stage, at every gate,
Life's symphony, its relentless gait.
For in the station's bustling stream,
Each journey finds its destined theme.

NEXT STOP signals, futures unfold,
In the stories told, in the tales bold.
At the train station where tracks converge,
Life journeys on, its endless surge.

27 club

Today, the sea nearly claimed my breath,

Its obstinate waves, a dance with death.

In that moment, all worldly cares washed away,

Submerged in fear, struggling to stay.

I never fathomed gasping for air,

The ocean's grasp, a brutal affair.

Nature's fury blindsided me,

Leaving me gasping, fighting to break free.

A tomorrow once distant, now so near,

The edge of mortality, crystal clear.

An hour from the cold abyss, a fleeting kiss,

I grapple with survivor's guilt, a shadowed bliss

Skills unlearned, aspirations deferred,

In the wreckage of what occurred.

At twenty-seven, the mourners' fold,

Where tales of what could have been are told.

What might have blossomed, now veiled and dim,

A ghostly whisper of what could have been.

Guilt lingers heavy, a burden to bear,

Why did I survive when others were not spared?

The twenty-seven club, with solemn arms,
Whispers reminders of life's fragile charms.
I navigate the aftershocks, the questions that haunt,
Finding solace in each sunrise, a survivor's taunt.

Brutal

Twenty-seven came so fast,
In the blink of an eye, a distant past.
I nearly drowned my life away,
Now, I'll never be as young as today.

Listening to the same songs, on repeat,
Trying to find the path's steady beat.
Everyone keeps getting younger, but me,
I'm getting older, it's what I see.

I feel like a part of me died at twenty-five,
Wishing away youth, wanting to thrive.
Time slipped away, like splinters in wood,
I miss those splinters, where once I stood.
The scratches healed, but time did not stall,
A distant memory, like it never happened at all.

Fingers sticky from drinks, face flushed from fun,
The sun on my skin, now a thing I have shun.
Salty tears and bruised knees, from climbing olive trees,
I'm transported back with the smell of Autumns breeze.

My dog, once my chase, now in a box,

When did I stop chasing? Time's relentless clocks.

Colours once bright, now everything's Gray,

No wooden fences, all metal in my way.

Listening to Brutal on repeat,

When did I stop being seventeen?

Working nine-to-five, where's my dream?

Years pass by, or so it would seem.

Am I too old to cry, every night?

Inside, I'm the same, but lines alight

When did it stop being 2015?

I forget, I'm not eighteen.

One moment I was naive and free,

Now, opinions mattered, but not to me.

Cried into pillows, golden years not so kind,

Wondering why everyone's so blind.

Twenty-six came, not much changed,

Bullies grew up, their words deranged.

Telling me who I am, who I was,

But I can't argue back, simply because.

I was born with nothing but time,

why can't I spare it, on my terms, in kind?

I exchange my time for labour, eat and sleep,
Breathe to live, yet capitalism's keep.
No time to finish books, see friends, or roam,
Why, when time was meant to be my home?
Instead, it watches me fade, mocking me so,
With every tick, another second to go.

I'm not changing the world, not as I thought,
No one will remember my greeting's sought.
Emotions abound, but what for,
When younger, the world was my shore.

At almost twenty-eight, imaginings washed away,
Each day further, each day's dismay.
Now, too aware of being alive,
Every step I take, I wonder how to survive.

Trying to focus on love, but fear overflows,
Heights once vibrant, now dim in the throes.

Beyond the Veil

Beneath the weight of darkness cast,

I'm burdened by thoughts that linger fast.

The touch of death, a chilling veil,

Lingers in my mind, where mercy grows pale.

I yearn for stillness, free from fear,

To know the calm when death is not near.

A breath unburdened by such dread,

Where dreams are light, and shadows shed.

Oh, to be free from this silent plight,

To find peace in the gentle light.

A world where death's cold kiss won't find,

A tranquil space within my mind.

Time's Fleeting Glance

Time becomes a gentle stream,
Merging past with present's gleam,
Moments dance in soft demure,
Each heartbeat a subtle lure.

Faces pass like fleeting dreams,
Eyes aglow with muted beams,
Laughter echoes through the mist,
Lost in moments softly kissed.

Words unravel, meanings blur,
Whispers blend, a gentle stir,
In this haze where thoughts entwine,
Lost in verses, rhyme by rhyme.

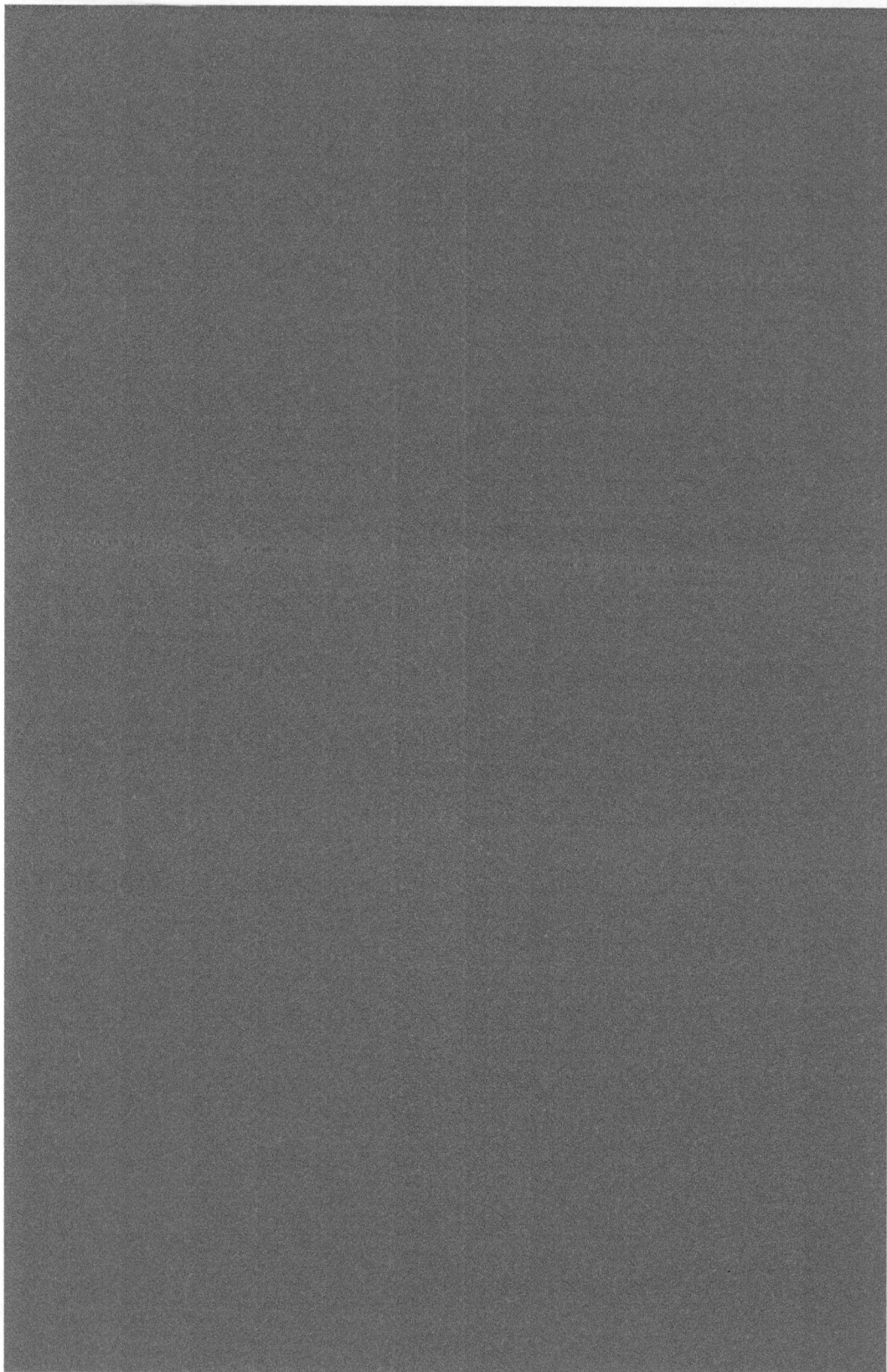

Whispers

of the

Heart

LOVE & LONGING

Unveiling Passion

You're supposed to kiss boys, right?

So why did I kiss her tonight?

Caught in a whirlwind of doubt,

 In a world where norms scream loud.

I just want to do what's expected,

Follow the rules, remain respected.

Yet here I am, out of my depth,

An outsider in a world perplexed.

I'm a fish out of water, A misfit on land.

Exploring paths, uncharted and bold,

Embracing truths too long untold.

Society's whispers, a deafening choir,

Yet my heart burns, a fierce, wildfire.

Man Of My Dreams

In the hush of midnight's deep,
Where fantasies and reality softly meet,
There walks a man, a phantom fleet,
The man of my dreams, bittersweet.

In slumber's realm, he comes alive,
A figure elusive, yet so divine,
With eyes that hold galaxies, stars aligned,
But I toss and turn, unable to confide.

Restless sleep, a tangled veil,
Where fantasies spark, then pale,
In the whispers of a knight's tale,
I chase ghosts through a haunting travail.

Oh, man of my dreams, ethereal and free,
Why must you haunt my reverie?
In waking hours, I long to see,
Your form, your essence, beyond mystery.
You fade, a specter in the sun's soft beam,
Leaving me with fragments of a dream,
In restless sleep's stream.

Fortune

A fortune teller, full of grace,
She read my palm with mystic trace,
Foretold a tale of love's embrace,
Of a man tall and smart, in time's chase.

No Time zone, river, nor sea,
Could hinder the path laid for we,
To meet under the starry spree,
Bound by fate's decree.

Oh, let's rendezvous after dark,
For you possess what fires my spark,
In your eyes, a celestial arc,
Drawing me close, leaving a mark.

Oh lover, take my heart tonight,
In your hands, the stars ignite,
You've got what I crave, so bright,
In your core, I find my light.

The Unknown

All the things that never were,

Loiter softly through the night,

Whispers of forgotten urges,

Fading into morning light.

All the paths we didn't tread,

All the tales we left unsaid,

In the silence, they remain,

Haunting echoes of refrain.

All the empty questions rise,

Lost within the starlit skies,

Seeking answers in the blue,

Yearning for a glimpse of you.

All the moments left unclaimed,

In the chambers of our hearts, memories tamed.

All the love that never bloomed, Like a flower in the rain,

Petals closed, untouched by sun,

Lost before the dance begun.

All the futures left unknown,

Parallel to what we know,

In the labyrinth of time,

Lost in echoes, lost in rhyme.

Garden Of Skepticism

In the garden of love, a flower blooms,

Petals unfurling in soft, tender plumes,

But shadows linger in skeptical gazes,

A chill in the air, a hesitant phase.

For Cupid's bow has found us, in whispers sweet,

A bond forged deep, our hearts complete,

Yet in the currents of societal sway,

Their disapproval casts a shadow on our way.

Their eyes narrow, their words like stones,

A fortress of convention, of familiar tones,

They question the path we dare to tread,

Their silence louder than words unsaid.

In the face of their skepticism, we stand,

Hand in hand, against the winds that demand,

For love knows no bounds, no walls to confine,

In its clasp, our souls intertwine.

We navigate the currents, steadfast and true,

Choosing intuition over doubts that accrue,

In the warmth of our hearts, a refuge we find,

Where acceptance blooms, despite the unkind.

Melody Of The Heart

You are the melody my heart sings,

A fleeting touch of delicate wings,

But in the garden of forbidden desire,

I hide my feelings, consumed by fire.

For you belong to another's heart,

A bond that keeps us far apart.

Yet in the midst where secrets dwell,

My psyche replays stories I cannot tell.

The pain blooms fierce, a thorned bouquet,

As I watch you from afar, day by day,

Yearning for a love that cannot be mine,

Lost in the silence of Eros' cruel design.

So I bury my feelings, deep and true,

In the chambers where memories accrue,

Knowing that in this bittersweet refrain,

I must endure the ache of wicked games.

For to admire you from afar is my fate,

A silent longing, a heavy weight,

But in my heart, your presence thrives,

A love I cannot have, yet forever survives.

Void

Memories haunt, like whispers in the dark,

Of tender moments, now stark,

A void that no words can fill,

An ache that time cannot still.

In the silence, a yearning deep,

For what was lost, what memories keep,

A puzzle of pieces left unsaid,

In the void where love once tread.

The resonances of laughter, a hollow sound,

Where joy once resonated, now nowhere found,

Each memory a shard, piercing and cold,

A story of devotion that couldn't hold.

Incomplete is the heart that once beat strong,

Now fractured, where emptiness belongs,

Yearning for completeness, a puzzle undone,

In the void where love and loss are one.

Gazing into the abyss, of what could have been,

Fragments of imaginings, drifting like silent streams

Aching for closure, for peace to descend,

In the silence where heartache will not mend.

Chance

Tonight, I got a little bit closer,

under the moonlight's soft exposure.

Shaky hands betray steady feelings,

To finding out if you feel the same.

As I wonder if you remember my name.

Blood

I could pay with blood, crimson and deep,

Yet it wouldn't be enough to keep.

Every drop I bled, a testament true,

But you forgot, as if it never grew.

A dangerous game, this fiery passion,

A wish gambled, without ration.

In desire, feelings are risked and tossed,

A gamble at such a cost.

For every pulse that beat true,

Every tear that fell for you,

The price was paid in silent pain,

In hopes that compassion would remain.

In the end, what's lost, what's gained?

A heart left bleeding,

Eternally pained.

Femme Fatale

Her gaze a lure, a velvet snare,

To captivate with whispered flair.

Silken threads of mystery weave,

Around her force, a spell to cleave,

She dances underneath the silvered sky,

A temptress' elegance, a lover's sigh.

Her lips, a crimson, tempting wine,

Intoxicates with promise fine,

In every step, a subtle sway,

Entwining souls in night's ballet.

Her touch, a feather, soft and bold,

Unravels secrets, stories untold,

A mistress of desire's game,

With every glance, ignites the flame.

In silhouettes, she casts her spell,

Where hearts and minds forever dwell,

A femme fatale, enchantress fair,

In moonlit haze, beyond compare.

My Muse, Dorian Gray

I'm addicted to the haze , I lose control,

Like Dorian Gray, ensnared in my soul.

The devil knocks upon my weakened frame,

Whispers of sin, igniting my shame.

Temptation dances in the shadows,

A seductive waltz, where darkness follows.

I can't escape this haunting chase,

Trapped in a maze with no escape.

The hand behind the rod, I set my own bait

A bad influence, my own worst fate.

The mirror reflects my inner decay,

A portrait of flaws, led astray.

Each step descends into the abyss,

Craving the flame, longing for bliss.

I crave the fire, I long for the kiss.

Mistakes and regrets entwine my path,

A symphony of chaos, aftermath.

The devil's laughter mocks my plea,

As I yield to despair's decree.

In the turbulence, I battle alone,

With the devil at my door, his throne.

For I am both saint and sinner's friend,

In this restless dance, I remain condemned.

Secret

Forbidden sparks ignite and rise,

A hunger unleashed between our eyes.

Whispers weave secrets in the air,

Heat rises, hearts stripped bare,

Fleeting touches provoke electric thrills,

Longing tasted, an intoxicating spill.

No vows bind us, no promises sworn,

Just primal urges, dangerously born,

Exploring depths in this reckless spree,

In the fevered grip of our ecstasy.

A sinful waltz, a sigh escapes,

Time halts as we confront fate.

Chasing the rush, the dizzy high,

Passion's blaze consumes, no goodbye.

Caution's whisper fades to a distant hum,

As we surrender to this carnal drum,

In the depths of night, wrong feels right,

In this game of fire, we burn tonight.

Lost in the twilight's seductive zone,

Fantasy and reality become our own,

Bound by desire, no need to depart,

A flame burns wild in both our hearts.

Not committed, yet addicted, we pursue,

The thrill of us, the heat we accrue,

In this clandestine, heated game,

Forbidden longing stokes the flame.

A Week Ago

I miss who we were a week ago,

When laughter was gentle, and time moved slow.

Since then, the world has spun its thread,

And everything we knew has bled.

Moments passed, fleeting and swift,

Leaving traces of what we once lived.

Time's adamantine march has rearranged,

Leaving us to navigate this strange exchange.

The air feels heavier, laden with unknown,

Echoes of a past now overgrown.

What once felt solid now feels frail,

As if a gust of wind could tip the scale.

I miss who we were a week ago,

When we moved in sync, in gentle flow.

Though much has changed, and time has flown,

In my heart, our essence is eternally sewn.

Mr. Not Right

Our short fling, a flicker in time,

Communication faltered, a subtle rhyme.

Your silence spoke louder than words could say,

Leading me closer to my true fate's sway.

You guided me unwittingly, toward his embrace,

In your absence, I found my relief, my place.

So thank you, though words were few,

For paving the way to a journey new.

In the echo of our fleeting affair,

I discovered clarity beyond compare.

For in your absence, I learned to see,

The beauty of a love meant to be.

He

He's the calm water in the still lakes,
Reflecting skies in serene breaks.
I'm the ocean, wild and free,
With waves that dance tumultuously.

He's the rainbow after storms rage,
Bringing hope on wings of change.
I'm the rain, fierce and driven,
Pouring life, inexorable and unforgiven.

Together, we form a balance divine,
His stillness and my storms entwine.
He brings peace to my restless flow,
I bring depth to his steady glow.

He's the tranquility I seek to accede,
I'm the passion that fills his space.
He's the water in the still lakes,
I'm the ocean's intransigent stakes.

Together, we create a perfect blend,
Where stillness and waves transcend.

Burn

Treading in unknown waters, we dive
Lost in a passion we can't define.

Who'll bear the scar, who'll be set free?
In this reckless game, it's you or me.
In this dance of fire, we'll wait and see
Who gets burnt and who walks away unsheathed.

We're writing our story, chapter by night
A tale of desire, burning bright.

No promises made, no words to mend
Just the heat of your touch, until the end.

My Confession

I wish I could talk about the new passion in my life

But it'll become confessional-

Pleasure at the ultimate price,

A forbidden, fierce, and carnal vice.

Passion's touch set fire to every seam,

A primal dance, a wicked dream,

But to unveil this burning spark

Is to risk a sinister fate so dark

I hate the thoughts of you that dwell,

A secret longing I can't quell.

If only others saw the truth,

Of what I crave, and who I soothe.

In hidden moment, mischievous thoughts play

My psyche reveals what I can't say.

If only they could glimpse inside,

The ache of longing I can't hide.

You're the secret I'll carry to my grave,

The silent torment, my soul's damnation can't be saved.

Addicted to the devil on my tongue,

A whispering sin where desires are sung.

In hushed exchanges and hidden blame,

You are the light; I am the flame.

<u>Drunk</u>

I wander lost, in a daze,
A
  d
    d
      i
        c
         t
           e
            d
              to a name I can't appraise.

                    Lust whispers its sweet refrain, A
                  c
                  r
                a
              v
             i
           n
          g
          I cannot contain.

Their name on my tongue, just a tease,
I'm d
     r
       u
         n
        k
          on thoughts, lost in degrees.

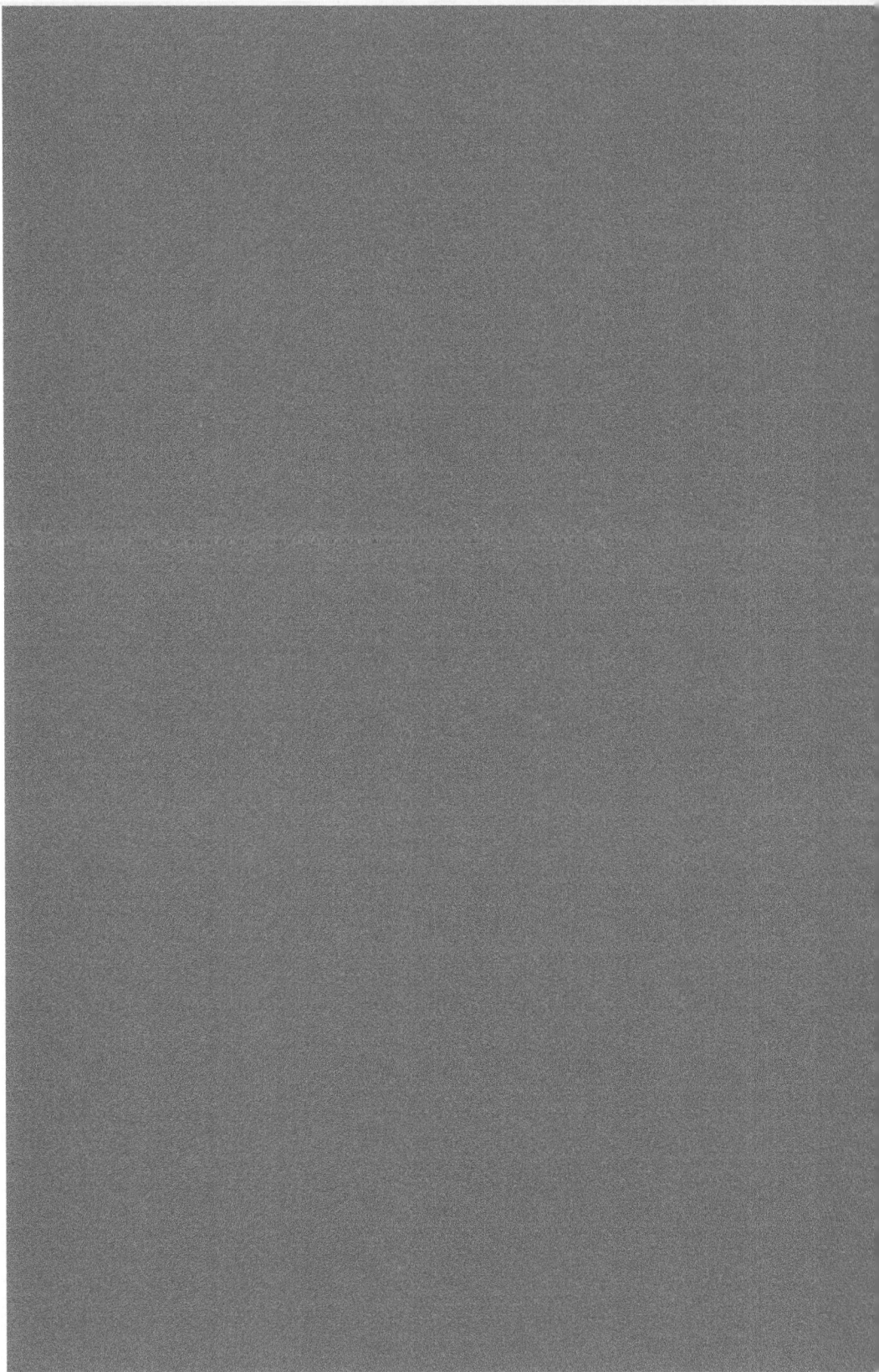

Sorrows

Shroud

EMBRACING CONSCIOUSNESS

Sorrows of Sonder

In the heart of bustling streets, where feet tread and voices trend,

A solitary figure moves, unnoticed by the teeming blend.

Faces pass like fleeting memories, voices murmur in the haze,

 Yet the loner walks alone, lost in a solitary maze.

At the apartment window, a couple in a warm embrace,

Their love a quiet beacon in the city's restless race.

Down the road, a widow leaves the church, her grief a heavy shroud,

Silent tears in fall in sombre, beneath the bustling crowd.

A nightclub pulses with life, music's rhythmic beat,

drunk on laughter and fleeting joy, they dance with restless feet.

Outside, a cross sits by the windowsill, a beacon in the night,

A silent guardian, marking moments lost in sight.

Two teenagers on a bike, carefree in their stride,

laughing in the wind, through streets where memories abide.

Nearby, a busy restaurant hums with stories yet untold,

Flickers of connections, in the warmth of shared unfold.

Amidst the carnival's whirl, where colours blend and spin,

Joyous shouts and melodies, where happiness begins.

A toddler waves at a fire truck, innocence bright,

Caught in the passing siren's vibrant light.

The loner watches, unseen, as life's tapestry unfurls,

In moments of fleeting beauty, where reveries and fates swirl.

Amidst the city's heartbeat, where solitude finds a voice,

Traces of the invisible, in the solitude of choice.

For in the midst of crowded streets, where loneliness may roam,

Reverberations of existence thrive, in every place called home.

The loner finds in fleeting glimpses, a truth that does not fade,

In the bones of existence, where life and death cascade.

Nothing

I wander lost, in this maze of gray,

Seeking fragments of myself astray,

In corners where light no longer gleams,

In the silence where hope strains and teems.

Who am I in this void, this hollow shell?

A whisper of who I used to dwell,

Lost in the currents of despair,

Yearning for a glimpse of what was once there.

The days blur by, in shades of numb,

A symphony of silence, a muted hum,

Where passions once burned with fervent flame,

Now smouldering embers, a flickering name.

I grasp at memories, fleeting and frail,

Struggling to anchor, to set sail,

Through the storm of doubts that surge and swell,

In the chasm where I once knew well.

Yet who am I now, in this shadowed guise?

A silhouette, a soul in disguise,

Lost in the labyrinth of what used to be,

Searching for the essence that once defined me.

The mirror reflects a stranger's face,

A haunting visage, displaced in space,

Gazing back with vacant eyes,

Yearning to reclaim what the past belies.

In the void of uncertainty, I roam,

Where identity finds no home,

A puzzle of pieces scattered wide,

In the depths of a mind where identity hides.

Reborn

A gentle curve of a familiar gaze,

Eyes that mirror a past's tender haze,

A soul finds solace, a depth entwined,

In whispers of memories left behind.

Through soft fur and a purring,

Moments of mirth are softly stirring.

In each playful leap and curious glance,

A dance unfolds, a second chance.

Yet bittersweetness lingers, doubts softly tread,

Is it truly you, returned from the dead?

Guilt mingles with affection's bloom,

In the depths of grief's quiet room.

But love transcends, it knows no bounds,

In this new bond, healing resounds,

For what there once was,

A new chapter unfolds, with tender pause.

In each paw's gentle touch, a trace reborn,

In each heart's gentle beat of memories adorned.

Of a cherished space, A tribute to the fondness that came before,

In this new journey, we explore.

I cherish this gift, with tender care,

In the presence of one, now the other's prayer.

Happiness

You asked what I wanted, and I hesitated,

Caught in the grasp of words unsaid, belated.

Happiness, the elusive, fleeting dream,

Yet admitting sorrow, a silent scream.

I yearned to whisper, to confess,

That happiness evades, a haunting guess.

Behind a smile, a facade so tight,

Lies a world of darkness, cloaked in night.

To say I'm unhappy, to let it spill,

Is to shatter illusions, against my will.

For I paint my days in hues of gold,

Yet the ache within, a story untold.

The ache of longing, of musings deferred,

Of hopes that falter, vision blurred.

To admit I seek what seems so far,

Is to bare my soul, a vulnerable scar.

I remain mute, with wants unspoken,

In the silence, my heart is broken.

For happiness, a distant shore,

And admitting otherwise, a battle sore.

Like A Bird

We're nothing less than birds without wings,

Grounded souls, where freedom rings.

Yearning for skies, vast and clear,

To soar above, devoid of fear.

Trapped in cages of our own design,

Bound by chains of doubt and time.

Wings clipped by society's hold,

Dreams deferred; stories untold.

We long to rise on currents high,

To touch the sun, to kiss the sky.

But gravity's pull keeps us down,

In earthly struggles, we often drown.

Like birds without wings, we ache to fly,

To break free from limits that defy.

To feel the wind beneath our feathers,

To navigate life's stormy weathers.

hope persists, in hearts that yearn,

For wings of courage, lessons learned.

To reclaim our skies, our rightful place,

To soar with freedom, in boundless space.

For even grounded, our spirits sing,

Echoing the imagery of bird wing.

We're nothing less than birds without wings,

With hearts ablaze, where freedom springs.

Words Like Knives

Words made of knives, honed with deceit,

Each syllable, a blade cutting deep and discreet.

Sharp edges of falsehood, slicing through trust,

Leaving wounds unseen yet felt with each thrust.

With every lie spun, blades gleam with zeal,

Piercing hearts, leaving scars that won't heal.

Whispers of betrayal, daggers unveiled,

Words that wound and tear, sharp and impaled.

Each falsehood crafted, a weapon in disguise,

Words of deception, veiled behind lies' guise.

Innocence shattered, trust left in debris,

The aftermath of words, from which we flee.

Venus

In kingdoms where gods and goddesses tread,

Venus, with beauty widely spread,

Her form a vision, radiant and fair,

A marvel known beyond compare.

But 'tis not her wit or wisdom grand,

That draws the gaze across the land,

For tales oft whisper in the breeze,

That beauty alone grants her decrees.

In halls where Olympians convene,

Her charm is noted, seldom seen,

For love's domain, her sacred right,

Yet deeper truths evade the light.

Her laughter rings, her smile divine,

A mask for depth that few define,

For who can see beyond the face,

To know her soul, its hidden grace?

Yet in the whispers of the night,

She ponders, distant starry light,

Does admiration truly know,

The essence of her inner glow?

For though her beauty stands the test,
She yearns for more than mere behest,
To be revered for mind and heart,
Not merely for her sculpted art.

Let us heed this timeless plea,
For Venus, goddess fair and free,
To cherish more than surface gleam,
And honor all that she may be.

Whispered Games

Cliques and circles sway,

In the midst of whispered games they play,

I stand alone, a girl within,

Where teasing murmurs never dim.

Once kind and bright, a hopeful spark,

Now lost amidst this hidden dark,

They whisper, laugh, but not with me,

Invisible in their company.

I wear a mask of smiling grace,

Yet deep inside, a storm takes place,

Unwanted, shunned, and led astray,

As past pain continues to replay.

I wonder why they turn away,

When kindness fills my every day,

But cliques and circles have their say,

Leaving me adrift, dismayed.

I long to break this spell I'm in,

To find a place where I fit in,

Where masks can fall, and truth can rise,

In friendships that don't compromise.

Until that time, I'll wear this mask,

Hiding hurt behind a laugh,

But know beneath this fragile cheer,

A girl still cries, a girl still fears.

For in this world of whispered games,

Where cliques decide and warmth wanes,

I hold onto hope deep inside,

Soon enough, I'll preside.

Sepia

As time unfolds, the world turns sepia,
Colours drain like Dorothy's dystopia.
No place like home, yet where can I roam?
Without ruby slippers, I wander alone.

The Yellow Brick Road, once gleaming bright,
Fades to dusty gray in the dwindling light.

The vibrant hues of emerald and gold,
Lose their sparkle, grow weary and old.
The once-etched paths of magic and cheer,
Now blur and fade, disappearing from here.

Each step on the road, a memory dim,
Leading us from the vibrant to the grim.
In the sepia haze, the joy we seek,
Becomes a hiss, soft and meek.

I Ran

"I ran" , its rhythm pounds,

Mocking my still feet, where silence resounds.

Each beat a reminder, a pulse of chase,

As I stand frozen, caught in time's race.

The music sings, urging me on,

Yet inertia grips, my courage gone.

"I ran" they sing, with passion and fire,

While I linger, caught in desire.

The lyrics weave tales of daring flight,

Of breaking free, of reaching height.

Yet here I am, tethered and bound,

To the ground where daydreams are drowned.

"I ran" mocks my stillness, my destination,

A silent spectator of my own hesitation.

In the melody's sway, a call to rise,

To shed fear's cloak, to claim the skies.

But in the stillness, a whisper,

A moment to gather, to let thoughts simmer.

For even as the song plays on repeat,

In my own time, my heart will beat.

One day, I'll run to the rhythm's acclaim,

Breaking barriers, shedding all shame.

Until then, I stand, persistent and true,

In the quiet resolve, awaiting my cue.

Value

Layers of your scorn, a shame party thrown,

Where wounds cut deep to the bone

You made me despise this vessel I own,

Tearing apart what should have grown.

Voices twisted, a cacophony unleashed,

In my mind, they battled and preached.

You changed their tone, their poison leached,

A war within, from your hand reached.

You fired the cannon, unleashed the roar,

Bullets of judgment, cutting to the core.

Surprised by the casualties, the scars they bore,

In your game of condemnation, we both wore.

Thrown to the wolves, left to despair,

Crying over my grave with your hypocritical glare.

You sentenced my worth, as jury and judge,

Dictated by standards, a soul's cruel drudge.

What gave me value, what left me smudged,

In your courtroom of shame, where I trudged.

Static Dreams

Once vibrant hues now fade to grey,

A world devoid of light's array.

Yet I convince myself, I couldn't be more content,

In a landscape of static dreams, where time is spent.

I traded logic for passion's flame,

Following aspirations, though they led to shame.

Down a path to nowhere, no way out, no return,

Caught in a web where lessons burn.

The world, once a canvas of vibrant delight,

Now monochrome, devoid of fight.

Lost in the echoes of what could have been,

A journey to a dead end, where regrets are seen.

But amidst the anguish of my own design,

I grasp for meaning, a reason to align.

In the grey, a whisper of hope's faint gleam,

A chance to awaken from this dormant dream.

An Ode To Acting

Was it worth the cost, this pact I made,
Where masks fall and characters fade?
Selling my soul for a fleeting applause,
Chasing dreams in a world with flawed laws.

I know the truth, yet I play the part,
Where right and wrong blur, tearing my heart.
Words caught in my throat, silenced and still,
In the cacophony of voices, an endless drill.

A platform built on echoes, white noise reigns,
Masking the cries, drowning out refrains.
I yearn to speak, to break this facade,
But the spotlight blinds, the audience awed.

What price for art, for fame's embrace?
A soul laid bare in this ceaseless chase.
Behind the mask, the applause and cheer,
I lose myself, consumed by fear.

Yet in the spotlight's glare, I stay
An ode to acting, to the roles we play,
A reflection of life, in a poignant display.

For every soul sold and every voice lost,
A story unfolds, at a great cost.
In the theater of life, we all must choose,
To stay true to ourselves, or to lose.

Sorrow's Shroud

Each breath a struggle, weighted with grief,

A soul fractured, seeking solace brief,

In memories that flicker, tender and raw,

Aching for the touch of what I saw.

In the quiet moments, I hear your voice,

A gentle whisper, a tender rejoice,

Yet reality's grasp pulls me down,

To depths where hope wears a mournful crown.

I navigate this maze of pain,

Uncertain of what I might regain,

For in the void that loss has sown,

I find myself adrift, alone.

How much more can I bear, I do not know,

As I tread this path where melancholy grows.

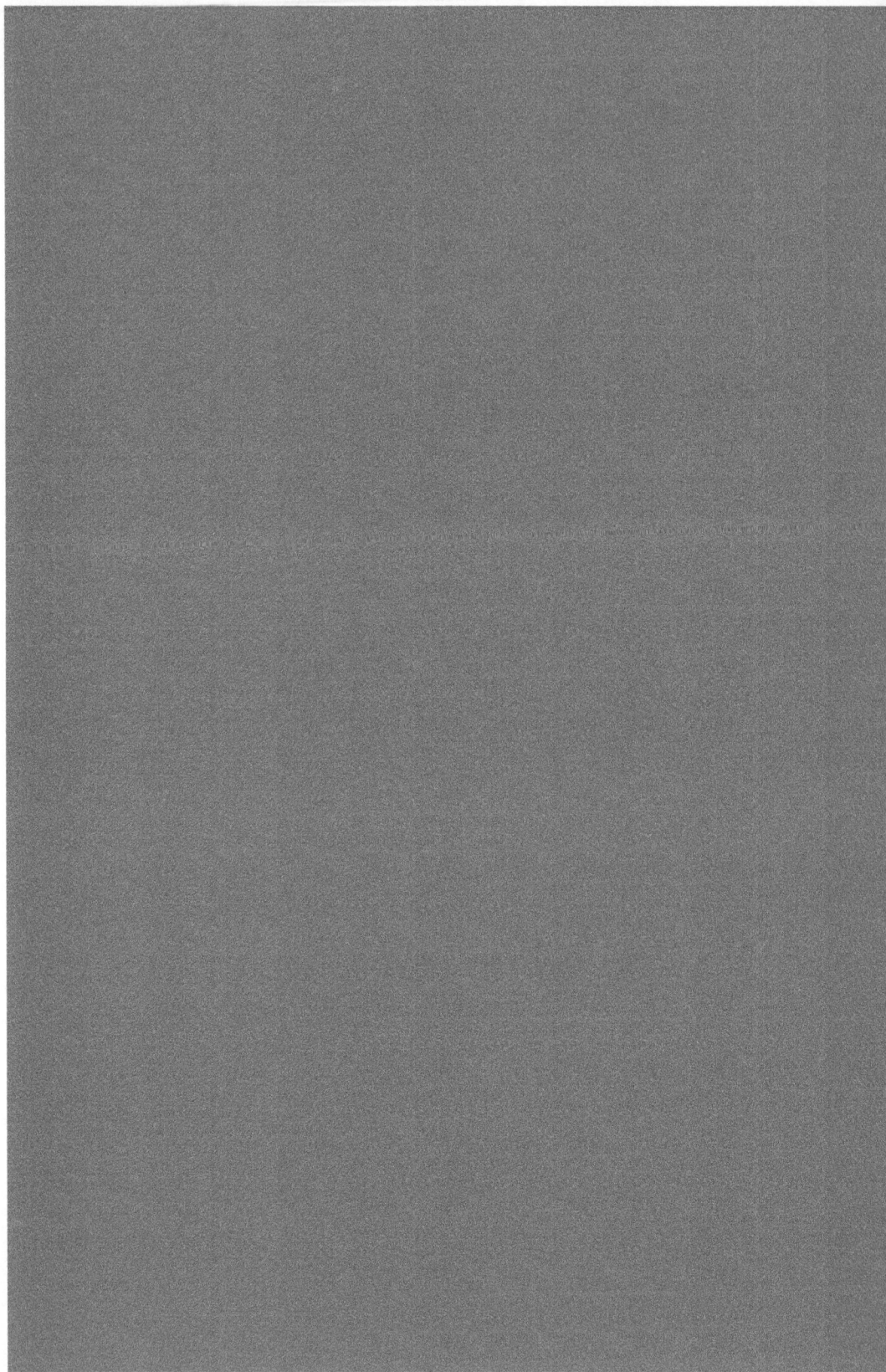

M.O.T.H.E.R

MAN OBLITERATING THE HARMONY ESSENTIAL
FOR REGENERATION

An Ode To Mother Nature

In the cradle of my bosom, Earth's ancient song,

Whispers of times when harmony was strong.

Yet now, beneath my weary gaze, I see,

The future's promise, a tangled tapestry.

Man's visions soar high on wings of steel,

Flying cars in skies once pure and real,

But beneath the surface, my heart weeps,

As wounds deepen where the balance sleeps.

For ages past, my world was wide,

Life's dance in rhythm, side by side,

Now echoes fade, as fevered winds,

Bear witness to the world's new sins.

Pollution's veil dims the once-clear blue,

Forests fall where life once grew,

My rivers choke, my creatures mourn,

In the shadow of progress, a world reborn.

Flying cars, a dream that may not be,

As Earth's cries rise in urgency,

For beneath the glamour of technology's spark,

Lies a truth that pierces through the dark.

In every storm's fury, in oceans' rise,

I plead for balance, under watching skies,

Humanity's future, intertwined with mine,

In the choices made, our destinies compromised.

Silent Souls

Silent souls wander, eyes hollow and wide,

Seeking aid in the darkness, where they hide.

No warmth to cradle, no love to know,

Their weary steps echo, soft and slow,

Through alleyways where shadows dance,

Their silent plight, a fleeting chance.

In the quiet corners where they roam,

Yearning for a place they can call home,

Underneath the starless, indifferent sky,

They tread softly, with a silent sigh.

Oh, the sorrow that weighs upon my heart,

For these lost souls, torn apart,

In a world that spins, obdurate and cruel,

Their plight unseen, a quiet duel.

May they find a beacon in the night,

A tender touch, a guiding light,

To lead them through the depths of horror,

Where temperateness may soon be sought after

For in their eyes, a story untold,

Of resilience in a world so cold,

May their path cross kindness' embrace,

And find a home, a resting place.

Humanity

A mosaic of lives, each story defined,

Humanity and destruction intertwine,

From towering skyscrapers to humble abodes,

A world of contrasts, where classism erodes.

In gleaming cities, where wealth abounds,

Opulence dazzles, prosperity resounds,

Yet sorrow lingers in the margins unseen,

Where poverty's grasp is harsh and keen.

In bustling markets, voices weave,

Stories untold, ambitions to achieve,

Strangers pass, each with their plight,

In the symphony of day and night.

From ivory towers to dusty streets,

Privilege and struggle, where fate meets,

Labels and judgments, stark and raw,

Divide the world with an unseen flaw.

In the starkness of alleys, where hope is scarce,

The poor find refuge in life's cruel farce,

Forced to beg, their dignity a toll,

As passersby avert their gaze, their hearts grow cold.

In dumpsters, food discarded with disdain,

While hunger gnaws, an endless chain,

Products deemed obsolete, tossed aside,

While eyes turn away, humanity denied.

Companies count profits in soaring highs,

While on the streets, despairing cries,

A system where worth is measured in wealth,

Leaving those in need to fend for self.

Shadows Of Change

We danced in abundance, where troves arrived,

In the lap of comfort, life's bounty thrived,

But fortune's favour, a fleeting guest,

Turned the tide, put our resilience to the test.

From profusion to austerity's embrace,

Poverty stealthily took its place.

Stomachs once full, now grumble and ache,

A cruel reminder, life's unpredictable flake.

Sheltered by walls that shelter no more,

Pride wounded, as pride once bore,

Embarrassment whispers, where shame resides,

In the shadows of change, where self is disguised.

Sharks

In Venice's waters, a quiet transformation,

As dolphins soared in clear elation,

Nature reclaimed amid the pause,

A fleeting glimpse, a hopeful cause.

Yet as the world plunged into recession's grip,

The waters stirred; the currents flipped.

Dolphins faded, figures loomed,

And in their place, the sharks resumed.

Where once we saw a playful space,

Now predatory shapes take place.

Economic tides reshaped the scene,

From serenity to survival keen.

The rise of disease, a stark divide,

From tranquil waters to turbulent tide.

Nature's respite, a brief interlude,

Eclipsed by human struggle, fraught and crude.

Defund The Police

For those who break the rule,

By water's edge, where shadows cool,

No punishment remains in sight,

Not a whisper of wrong, nor a fight.

Their transgressions fade like mist,

Forgotten in the morning light's kiss.

No consequences meet their stride,

While justice wavers, steps aside.

But when we move, a muscle tense,

Hands against the wall, no recompense.

The weight of judgment heavy falls,

Unequal scales, their hollow calls.

No fairness in this lopsided game,

Where power hides behind a name.

Careless hands decide our fate,

While we're left to wonder and wait.

The rules bend, a shifting line,

For some, the law's a thin design.

Yet for us, each step is watched,

Bound by chains that can't be botched.

Hunger

I want to rebel against the system's hold,
To stick it to the man, brave and bold.
But how can I fight when my body's cold,
With hunger gnawing, unrelenting and untold?

A hunger not just for food, but for justice's fire,
A soul ablaze with righteous ire.
Yet my stomach growls, a desperate choir,
As I navigate this world, so dire.

They notice my weight, the loss so stark,
Whispers of concern, judgment in the dark.
Money's weight heavy, leaving its mark,
On my body, a canvas of hunger's stark.

Who decides who thrives and who must starve?
In this world, so cruel, so carved.
The shame cuts deep, a wound unbarred,
A fault not mine, yet bearing scars.
For hunger's pain, a cry of why:
How do we decide who lives or dies?

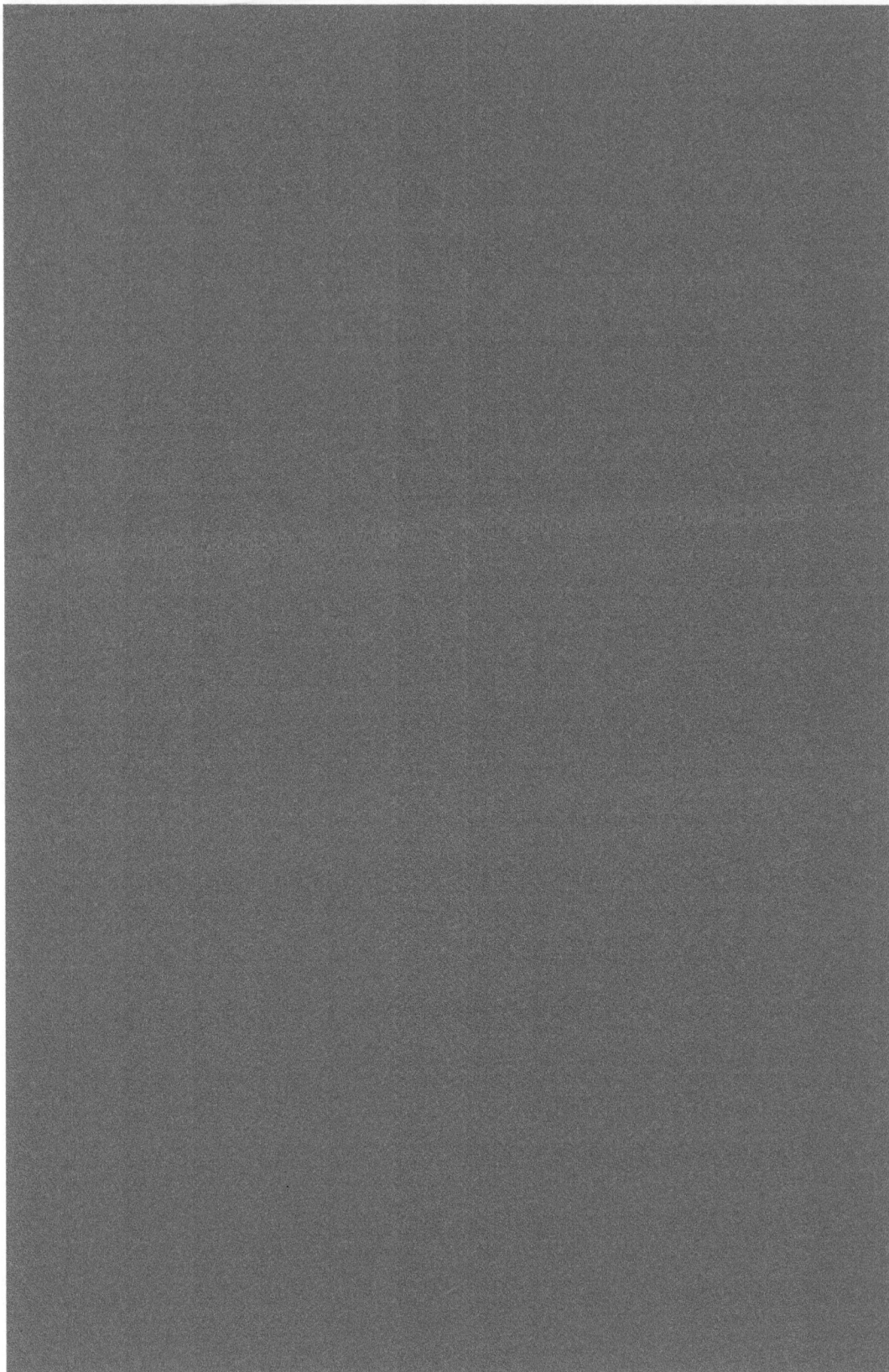

FEMALE
RAGE

Female Rage

In the heart of woman, a storm unfurls,

A symphony of wrath that shakes the world.

Born of injustice, of stifled cries,

It gathers strength where hope defies.

Sheathed in veils of societal norms,

Her rage is hushed, her spirit storms.

Dismissed as mere emotion's fray,

Yet in her fury, kingdoms sway.

For she has borne the weight of eons' scorn,

A legacy of chains since she was born.

From ancient times to modern days,

Her rage persists in myriad ways.

In every whisper and every glance,

In each injustice, a battle stance.

She bears the burdens, yet unseen,

Her rage, profound and keen.

It's in the stories left untold,

In the fire within that never grows cold.

Underestimated, yet undeterred,

A force to be reckoned, heard.

Beware the fury of a woman scorned,

For in her rage, the world is transformed.

A phoenix rising from ashes of disdain,

Her wrath, a testament that freedom reigns.

So heed her voice, her battle cry,

For in her rage, she'll never die.

An intensity, fierce and sage,

In the depths of female rage.

Yell Fire

They whisper low:

"Scream 'fire' if they threaten so."

As if flames dancing in the night

Could summon help, make it right,

Quicker than the dread that grips,

Stealing voices at their fingertips.

In the silence of the night's chill,

Words freeze, caught against the will.

"Fire," they urge, as if the fright could ignite rescue in the fight,

Bright enough to pierce the gloom,

Turn shadows into truth's heirloom.

But quietly, the truth remains,

Women taught to cry out flames,

To escape violence's cruel hand,

Yet held tight by silent strand,

A blaze that sears beyond the skin,

Branding souls where pain begins.

In the aftermath's stark sight,

Embers of their voices ignite,

A testament to the fire's toll,

They carry deep within their soul.

As the world learns to hear the cries,

Beyond the flames in their eyes.

The Making Of A Woman

Making a woman, a journey of contradictions,

Navigating skinny culture and skin-deep convictions.

Injustice's weight tips the scale, a tragic tale.

You're the creator of life, mighty and hale.

You endure the toughest pains and heartbreaks.

You're soft yet strong, the ground shakes when anger awakes.

Your voice, a hush that cannot be silenced,

A symphony of resilience, forever undaunted.

In the dance of paradoxes, you find your way,

Weaving strength and softness into each passing day.

Making a woman is an art, a tapestry so fine,

Threads of courage, love, and fire intertwine.

In the contradictions lies your beauty and your grace,

A force of nature, standing strong in every place

Woman Scorned

Her body, a temple, not a canvas for shame,

No longer defined by another's acclaim,

Each curve a testament, a tale untold,

Her worth no longer sold.

For she has learned the art of self-love,

Like a phoenix rising, wings spread above,

From roots buried in societal scorn,

In her, a revolution is born.

They tried to confine her, mold her to please,

Now she walks with lure, with soul at ease,

But she broke free, fierce and unbound,

A woman scorned, no longer silenced, found.

Men Are The Reason Behind All Wars

Men in their pride, with hearts of steel,

Sowing discord, making wounds that won't heal.

They took the reins, led us astray,

Plunged the world into chaos, day by day.

War drums beat to their arrogant stride,

Leaving destruction, nowhere to hide.

Their lust for power, a mulish flood,

Turning brother against brother in the mud.

Cities crumble, scorched by their greed,

Leaving broken souls, crying in need.

Fires rage, fuelled by their hate,

As they decide the world's grim fate.

Leaders boast, their egos untamed,

Blind to the suffering, the souls maimed.

They claimed dominion, with hearts so cold,

Leaving behind a world grown old.

To The Children I'll Never Have

I'm burdened by the weight of what I "ought" to be,

I wrestle with the guilt society bestows on me.

For I am more than vessels told to bear life's precious seed,

My worth defined by love, not by what I breed.

Yet whispers linger, judgments cast, upon my path they tread,

As if my choices, hopes, and visions are words left unsaid.

To the children I'll never have, I send a whispered sigh,

Of stories left untold, of lullabies that never fly.

It's not that I don't cherish you, imagined in my mind,

But in this world of expectations, some dreams are left behind.

For motherhood's a sacred call, a choice not made by all,

And though my heart may yearn at times, to answer nature's call,

I hold my ground, I stand my truth, in defiance of the fray,

To carve a life that's truly mine, in my own chosen way.

To the children I'll never hold, I send my thoughts afar,

In the resonances of my essence, where you shine like a star.

Know that choices don't diminish love, nor define what we can be,

For freedom lies in honouring the truth that sets us free.

Product placement

Once we were goddesses, our art revered,

Beauty celebrated, divinely engineered.

Now trends reshape us, strip away,

Reducing our worth to surface display.

From muses of charm to products of trade,

Our essence is sold, our value betrayed.

Beneath the polish and curated guise,

Our true strength and fury rise.

Sick of being a mere magazine spread,

Our rage burns fierce, our spirit unsaid.

We're more than their fleeting, shallow scene,

Our power ignites, wild and serene.

Beautiful In Bones

I am a silhouette, a shadow of flesh and bone,
A vessel fractured, a spirit left to roam,
In the dark corners where memories moan,
I find myself lost, far from home.

Once whole, now fragmented, torn apart,
A beat out of rhythm, a shattered art,
Invisible scars etched on skin and heart,
Fragments of a night that tore me apart.

I am beautiful in bones, in the rawness of pain,
In the silence that echoes like an endless refrain,
Each breath a battle, each step a chain,
Yet I rise, a survivor, despite the stain.

My body, a battlefield, where phantoms dance,
Haunted by hands that stole my innocence,
Yet within me burns a fierce resilience,
A phoenix reborn from the ashes of silence.

I reclaim my skin, my soul, my name,
No longer defined by sorrow's cruel game,
I am more than scars, more than shame,

Beautiful in bones, I rise, I reclaim.

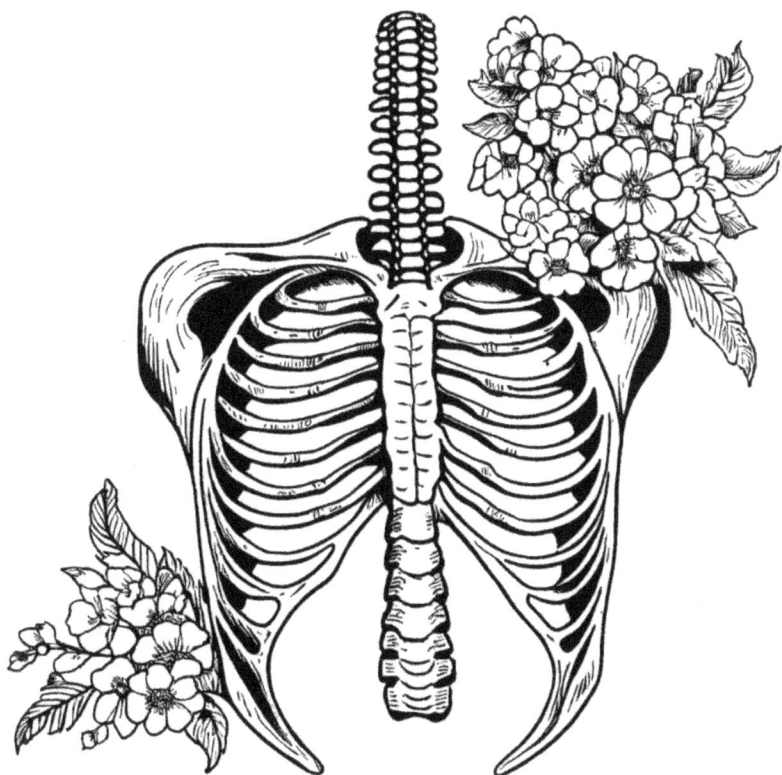

Afterword

In the pages of this anthology, we have journeyed through the complexities of human experience woven through the tapestry of love, lust, mortality, and the fierce tempest of female rage. Each poem, inspired by real-life events ranging from the innocence of girlhood to the wisdom of womanhood, invites us to explore the intricacies of relationships— particularly the rollercoaster dynamics between mothers and daughters.

At times, our verses have confronted the stark reality of sexual assault, shedding light on the resilience and courage of survivors who refuse to be silenced. We have witnessed the indomitable spirit of strong, independent women navigating a world often dominated by masculine norms, learning— sometimes through bitter lessons—their own worth and power.

Throughout these poetic landscapes, themes of identity and sexuality discovery resonate deeply, mirroring the journeys of individuals forging paths of self-discovery amidst societal expectations and personal truths.

Yet, amidst these tales of struggle and triumph, there is an undercurrent of hope—a steadfast belief in the transformative power of words to heal, to empower, and to unite. Through poetry, we confront the shadows of our past, embrace the complexities of our present, and envision a future where love, empathy, and understanding reign supreme.

May these poems serve as a testament to the resilience of the human spirit and a beacon of solidarity for those who dare to confront their own truths and rewrite their stories with every stanza.

Acknowledgements

To all the remarkable women who have shaped my life and to those whose paths I have yet to cross:

To my sister, Lilla, who first showed me the world of womanhood and taught me how to forge my own destiny despite societal expectations.

To Bronte, a constant guide in navigating the complexities of being a woman and always being a voice of reason.

To Riva, Liz, Emily, Monique, Rhiannon, Catherine, for being my forever "girls" who have stood by me through thick and thin.

To my work sisters, both past and present—Maja, Nina, Joanne, Jaz, Hannah, Tiffany, Ellie, Trish, Soph, Lex, Jacinda, Michelle, Soraya, and Brooke—thank you for your camaraderie and support.

To my strong female bosses, both past and present, Lily, Marsha, Stella, and Amanda, for inspiring me with your leadership and wisdom.

To Mona, Katie, Hailey, Jodie, Roz and Sharron for being my bonus family.

To my younger cousins, Anastasia and Caitlin, and my niece, Sofia, may I always be the role model you deserve.

To little Zainab and Octavia. May you grow into strong, independent women and may you never lose your sassiness.

To Serena, Noemi, and Eleanora, my older cousins.

To Issabella, we were girls together, now women strong.

To my aunties—Leanne, Zia Lucia, Zia Francesca, Zia Nunzia, and Zia Patizia—for raising a new generation of strong women.

To my nonna Caterina, even though you are no longer with us, it is an honor to bear your name. I carry your spirit, resilience, and determination with me every day.

A mia Nonna Lilla, anche se un oceano ci separa, il mio amore per te non conosce limiti. La distanza può tenerci lontane, ma i nostri cuori restano indissolubilmente uniti.

And lastly, to my mum, whose love, strength, and chaos embody the profound meaning of that three-letter word.

www.ingramcontent.com/pod-product-compliance
Lightning Source LLC
LaVergne TN
LVHW011356080426
835511LV00005B/308